Psychological Assessment Recommendations... simplified

Psychological Assessment Recommendations... simplified

Phillip D. Snyder Ph.D.

Dedication

For Cindy, Joe, James and Amy

Contents

Preface

The ultimate goal of Psychological Assessment is to provide answers to perplexing clinical questions for professionals and ultimately to help the test subject in some way—psychologically, emotionally, physically or developmentally. If this is not the case than why do we conduct psychological assessments in the first place? Therefore, when the testing is over and the results are in, the most important question a doctor or parent can ask is," Now what do we do?"

This book was written to fulfill the need for a quick reference guide for clinicians who may need help with treatment recommendations. While supervising graduate Psychology students for the past 25 years I recall many of them saying over and over again, "If I had only known what recommendations to make." Therefore while researching and writing this book I found many helpful assessment report recommendations that are included in this book and many more that can be added in later revisions. This book provides a current review of psychological assessment recommendations in a compact, time saving, easy to read format.

With psychological assessment we proceed with the assumption that knowledge is power. The more we know about psychological test results and treatment recommendations per clinical problem, the more we are able to make intelligent and sound choices. Ultimately, the test subject or parent will decide which treatment option works best for them.

I hope this book can be one tool to help you make your way through the complicated task of psychological assessment.

Phillip Snyder, Ph.D.
2012

A Word to Professionals

It is my hope that mental health professionals, school counselors, teachers, speech and language clinicians and all health providers will use this book as a tool to help them through the psychological assessment report with suggestions that offer an opinion or recommendation relevant to the referral question. These recommendations should never be used verbatim but should be customized as a set of statements to support your final decision or recommendation. The recommendations that you provide should summarize the material presented in the body of the psychological assessment report, and should not contain new interpretations. This book is practitioner oriented with easy-to-read treatment recommendations. It is written in a nonacademic style and formatted as an ongoing quick and easy reference.

I am well aware that a book of this nature merely scratches the surface of the conclusion and recommendations of the assessment process. However, I also realize that there is not enough information available to mental health clinicians that provide even the most basic discussion of test recommendations and all its ramifications.

Recommendations

AA or NA

1. Xxx is in need of ongoing treatment for her substance abuse problem. A group approach such as AA or NA is recommended. Xxx is very likely to relapse, given her poor self-esteem and her resistance to look at the factors which contribute to her sense of inadequacy and substance abuse in the past.

2. Xxx alluded to her past drug involvement, but claimed to be sober for about a year. It would be important to support her sobriety. Furthermore, given that she often avoids dealing with personal problems and tends to deny or minimize disturbing issues, she may be at risk for engaging in periodic drug involvement. It would be important to explore with Xxx whether she is amenable to attending such groups such as AA or NA so that she can maintain her current level of adjustment.

3. Xxx's chemical dependency issues need to be evaluated further. He should be considered for receiving CD treatment which is offered by NA, AA, ACA etc. Discuss these options with him and assist him in getting the help he needs.

4. Xxx alluded to recent use of cocaine. It would be important to evaluate his chemical dependency involvement and take appropriate actions.

Academic or Vocational Training

5. Xxx expressed pride in her more recent academic achievements and seemed to have a genuine interest in pursuing academics more than she has in the past. Given what appears to be above-average intellectual ability, it would

be important to encourage her to focus her efforts in the area of academics. Thus, outlets for these feelings and desires should be supplied.

6. Given her age, it is important for Xxx to clarify her education, vocational, and social objectives. She needs help in learning how to set realistic goals, implementing a plan and sustaining her motivation until her aims are achieved.

Anger Management and Conflict Avoidance

7. Xxx needs to examine and revise his means for identifying and resolving conflict. Attempts on his part to deny, avoid and project should be identified and alternative ways of responding should be explored.

8. Anger Management counseling may be helpful to teach Xxx more adaptive ways to assert herself and gratify her needs. Furthermore, she needs to learn to comply with authority figures without feeling threatened or otherwise demeaned.

9. Xxx clearly needs to develop skills in terms of managing his anger. Assertion training is strongly recommended as a means of ventilating his anger and resolving conflicts with others. Additionally, any type of physical outlet, such as sports or exercise may be helpful in reducing his anger.

10. Modeling and encouragement of more direct, moderated expression of feelings would be helpful. She needs to become more aware of the possible triggers for her anger and how to direct her hostility to appropriate outlets. She would benefit from understanding that her anger, at times, is really a reflection of underlying feelings of hurt, disappointment and possible anxiety that she has a difficult time expressing openly. Attempts on Xxx's part to deny, project, minimize, rationalize, or act-out should be identified, and alternative ways of responding be discussed.

11. Xxx should be assisted in examining the underlying sources that trigger his hostile outbursts. It is important that he begin to realize that his anger is multi-functional and may reflect the expression of underlying feelings and affect

that are threatening for him to openly acknowledge. He would benefit from learning cognitive behavioral techniques that would help him raise his threshold and better manage his agitation.

12. Xxx needs to be assisted in examining the underlying sources and triggers for her angry responses. She would benefit from learning CBT techniques to raise her overall threshold and increase her ability to manage her stress and anger. It is important that she learn to identify, as well as accept, the fuller range of her feelings including her vulnerable emotions. Treatment staff can model as well as encourage more open, moderated expressions of these feelings.

13. Xxx would benefit from understanding what triggers his angry responses and to learn how to direct his hostility more appropriately. He would benefit from understanding that his anger, at times, is really a reflection of underlying feelings of inadequacy.

Assertiveness Training

14. It is important for Xxx to learn how to assert himself and gratify his needs in a more mature, direct fashion. Assist him in being able to accept himself with his peers, and in setting appropriate limits in his interactions with them.

15. It is important that Xxx learn how to assert herself in a non-defiant fashion. Her angry outbursts have created difficulties for her in the past. She needs to find other, verbally oriented ways to express her needs and make her positions known. In turn, it is important that she learn how to set appropriate limits as well as accept the limitations of others when dealing with peers and adults alike.

16. Xxx clearly needs to develop skills in terms of managing his anger. Assertiveness training is strongly recommended as a means of ventilating his anger and resolving conflicts with others.

17. In order to reduce anger, role playing or rehearsal of adaptive (as opposed to maladaptive) ways of coping with an-

ger, can help reduce his involvement in physical alterca-
tions.

18. Xxx needs to be able to assert herself and vent her emotions in a less verbally hostile fashion. Her tendency to
"mouth off" remains a problem. Role playing and modeling may be helpful in providing her with behavioral and
cognitive tools that assist in controlling her aggression.

Attention Deficit Hyperactivity Disorder

19. In the school setting a behavioral program which uses
time out for hyperactive behaviors should be implemented to reduce the intensity and increase Xxx'x chances of
comprehending and attending to the materials presented. If this behavior is also present within the home setting
a similar program of "time out" should be implemented.

20. In home situations, it would be helpful to set goals and
consequences for inappropriate and excessive motor behavior. Time-out or response cost (loss of points), consistently applied, may reduce her hyperactivity and support
the effects of her medication, and help her develop a
sense of self-control and mastery of hyperactivity.

Art Therapy

21. A dream journal and art therapy might also be helpful in
assisting Xxx to confront internalized sources of anguish.
Art techniques would offer a medium which would enhance Xxx's expressiveness.

22. Because Xxx has difficulties expressing herself verbally
and tends to withhold information and feelings, adjunc-
tive therapies such as art and bibliotherapy may be helpful.

Behavioral Counseling

23. Behavioral counseling can train parents and teachers to
use consistent patterns of punishment and reward.

24. Providing Xxx with behavioral learning and feedback would be of great benefit. Providing him with the opportunity to learn and practice these skills as well as giving him consistent feedback would enable him to learn and practice these skills and help him to develop more age-appropriate skills.

25. Xxx repressed her traumatic social history, which combined with limited intellectual ability, offers a prognosis which must be considered guarded. Interventions might therefore rely more heavily on behavioral prescriptions which offer her social skills and behavioral alternatives in dealing with family members and peers alike.

26. Xxx is in need of a concrete, behaviorally oriented, structured approach that consistently will reinforce both his positive and negative behaviors in order to promote a linkage between consequences and behaviors.

27. A strong behavioral approach utilizing clear, specific limits with Xxx is clearly indicated. Further, the use of logical consequences is indicated, with feedback to assist Xxx regarding the consequences of her behavior so she can better gain a sense of cause and effect relationships.

Behavior Modification

28. Xxx needs clear and consistent rules and guidelines for his behavior. A concrete, behaviorally oriented, structured approach that consistently reinforces his positive and negative behaviors will promote a sense of security and control.

29. Contingency management could help reduce disruptive behavior. By identifying valued reinforcers which might include games, sports, internet, TV, or social reinforcers, could be used as a reward for desired behavior.

30. Xxx should be placed in a highly structured setting which provides a strong behavior modification program and staff who are able to interact in a warm and accepting way. Xxx continues to need a concrete behaviorally oriented structured approach that will appropriately reinforce her posi-

tive and negative behaviors in order to promote a linkage between consequences and behavior.

31. Management of specific inappropriate behaviors is recommended, using a system that requires the desired behaviors to be specified clearly. Xxx'x performance on these behaviors needs to be carefully recorded, and successful performance systematically and consistently rewarded.

Bibliotherapy

32. Bibliotherapy assignments related to ACA and Co-Dependency topics may be important adjuncts to Xxx'x current psychotherapy.
33. Xxx'x mother is alcoholic. He might benefit from exposure to literature or a self-help group designed to address the concerns of individuals from alcoholic families.

Big Brother / Big Sister

34. Xxx has lacked exposure to consistent, positive nurturing role models. He needs to gain exposure to both males and females in a more rewarding, nourishing fashion than has occurred up to this point in time. Thus he might find it useful to form an attachment to an adult who does not act in a position of authority over him. It should be considered whether he might be a viable candidate to have a volunteer from some organization such as the Big Brothers. This type of bond might serve as a surrogate parental figure that Xxx longs for, but has not been able to enjoy.
35. If feasible, it should be explored whether Xxx is amenable to possibly participating in some program where she has an opportunity to bond with an adult female. She might be a good candidate for the Big Sisters program where she would have an opportunity to form a consistent, exclusive relationship with an older female.
36. Fostering Xxx's relationship with a strong, masculine role model might be considered given his negative identification with his father.

37. Xxx might benefit from a mentoring relationship. She reports that she desperately wants to have a special friend. This special friend might be someone who can provide her with a positive role model.

Bizarre Behaviors

38. It has been suggested that Xxx may manifest bizarre types of thinking and responding under conditions of prolonged stress. It is difficult to diagnose with certainty that she is psychotic because of the questionable reliability of the current test findings. However staff should be alert to the possible emergence of psychosis. At that time, psychiatric evaluation would be helpful with the adjunct use of psychotropic medications to promote greater behavioral and emotional control.

39. Because this individual is delusional and is experiencing a sense of helplessness and hopelessness which render her quite depressed, her suicidal ideations and or attempts need to be addressed.

Boyfriend / Girlfriend

40. Xxx seems highly reliant on her attachment to her boyfriend to provide her with the security, support etc. that she does not necessarily experience with peers or family members. While this can be a positive experience for Xxx, she may be overly reliant on this relationship to feel steady and secure. Assist Xxx in being realistic in her expectations of this relationship and encourage her to find additional means of feeling nurtured and worthwhile.

Cognitive Techniques

41. Xxx would benefit from training in a broader range of coping strategies to help him manage his emotions when they surface. These might include cognitive control techniques, learning to ask for help or comfort, and learning

to express emotions verbally. These might be supplied through individual or group psychotherapy.

42. Providing Xxx with the behavioral learning and feedback that is necessary to put her feelings into words, rather than acting them out, would be of great benefit. It appears she has been rewarded in the past for immature behaviors and has not learned or been rewarded for more age appropriate behaviors. Providing the opportunity to practice social skills, as well as giving her constant feedback, would help bring them to a more age-appropriate level.

43. Encourage him to verbalize or write down alternative choices and possible outcomes. In this way he will become more aware of the ramifications of his decisions.

44. Staff modeling and encouragement of more direct and moderated expression of emotions, including Xxx's fears, self-doubts and sadness are recommended. He would benefit from becoming more comfortable with this aspect of his personality and emotions.

45. Xxx needs to be assisted in examining the underlying sources and triggers for his angry responses. He would benefit from learning Cognitive Behavioral techniques to raise his overall awareness of his emerging anger and provide him techniques to defuse and appropriately manage his anger.

46. Conflict resolution strategies can help Xxx learn to negotiate, defuse, avoid or appropriately confront problematic interpersonal interactions.

47. Xxx needs to be able to assert herself and appropriately vent her emotions in a less verbally hostile fashion. Her explosiveness remains a problem. Role playing and modeling may be helpful in providing her with behavioral and cognitive tools that assist in controlling her aggression.

Elopement Risks

48. No specific intent to run away was suggested by the testing material. However, given Xxx's background, she may engage in this type of behavior. It would be important for

treatment staff to work with Xxx to identify alternative ways to cope should the urge to run away arise.

49. Xxx is a risk for possibly running away from the facility. He does manifest some capacity for self-control. Furthermore, on some level he recognizes that he can't return home and is in need of a placement until he can emancipate. However, dealing with the emotions evoked within his placement on a daily basis can sometimes be overwhelming for him. It would be important for him to find alternative ways to deal with these feelings when they do arise.

Emancipation

50. Issues concerning Xxx's emancipation need to be specifically addressed. The idea of emancipation may evoke longstanding issues of separation and loss given her background. She does have the capacity to be self-sufficient, however, emotional factors may block her ability to feel more successful. Within the counseling session, it would be important for her to explore her issues regarding her current circumstance and the implication of her emancipation on longstanding issues of separation and loss.

51. Given his age and current circumstance, Xxx is in considerable distress about his anticipated emancipation. He is confused and finding it difficult to identify his educational, vocational and social objectives. He needs assistance learning how to set realistic goals, implementing a plan, and sustaining his motivation until his aims are achieved.

52. Since he will do best in structured environment, his aspirations to join the Air Force upon achieving adulthood may be quite realistic. He is certainly intelligent enough to do well in any number of Air Force career fields.

53. Given her age, it is important that she be assisted in clarifying her educational, vocational, and social objectives. She needs help in learning how to set realistic goals, implementing a plan, and sustaining her motivation until her aims are achieved.

54. She should be encouraged to continue working, as employment may increase her self esteem, as well as help her toward her goal of becoming, what she sees, as successful in business.

55. Xxx should begin to discuss careers, and explore his interests and expectations of the future. He appears to be a good candidate for an Interest Inventory battery of tests.

Family Therapy

56. Xxx continues to feel a sense of closeness with her parents even though she is filled with a sense of anger. If Xxx continues to involve her parents in her life, it may be appropriate at some future date to initiate family counseling and gradually work toward a reunification plan.

57. If there is a possibility of reunification in the future, family therapy should be instituted in order to work through past conflicts between Xxx and his parents to work toward possible reunification.

58. Family therapy will be important to help the parents learn how to set effective limits and consequences with Xxx. Therapy could help Xxx learn how to directly express his feelings to his parents and in general heal the distorted family communication patterns that have been established.

59. Family issues seem to be a central part of Xxx's emotional problems. She needs to gain a greater understanding about how her feelings in reference to her mother may have interfered with her adjustment to her step-mother. If possible, family work would be advisable. Xxx would benefit from understanding how these early experiences have influenced her self-esteem, coping strategies, and interpersonal relationships.

Fire Setting

60. Xxx's preoccupation with fire needs to be specifically addressed. It was unclear from the current test findings the severity of Xxx's fire-setting ideations. However, there

does seem to be some potential for Xxx to engage in this type of behavior in the future. It would be important to explore with Xxx the meaning behind, and possible impact of, his fire-setting. He needs to find alternative ways to cope with those emotions that are being evoked that have typically led to his preoccupation with fire in the past.

Foster Parents

61. Xxx's foster parents should be encouraged to take a behavioral management class that will equip them with greater skill in managing Xxx'x difficult behavior.
62. Xxx'x foster parents should be encouraged to take a behavioral management class that will equip them with greater skill in managing her difficult behavior. Therefore when Xxx becomes obstinate, her foster parents might try addressing the underlying emotion by acknowledging it. When Xxx is being particularly oppositional, her foster parents might try saying,"I wonder if you're worried about something now." This might offer Xxx an opening for her to talk about her feelings. Knowing that her foster parents understand her, regardless if she responds directly to their statements, will promote feelings of security and safety.

Gangs

63. Xxx spoke of continued identification and affiliation with a gang. It is essential that Xxx learn how to feel good about himself and interact with others in a non violent or gang oriented fashion. He has clearly identified with the values and norms of his major reference group. He needs to build a more independent identity and enhance his understanding of societal conventions so that he can relate more appropriately with the world in ways that do not violate typical standards of conduct.
64. Xxx needs to attend her school sponsored seminar on bullying prevention and ways to avoid being victimized by others.

Group Therapy

65. Xxx would benefit from being involved in group therapy to help him to begin to establish and maintain social interaction. The group should be initially supportive and not confrontational.
66. Group or milieu therapy with peers would be helpful to assist in developing age-appropriate interpersonal interactions, problem-solving, decision-making and behavior.
67. Group or milieu therapy with age related peers is recommended for Xxx to focus on development and practice of adequate social skills, increase adequate problem solving skills and to learn to inhibit behavior that is harmful or unacceptable to others.
68. Xxx would benefit from individual as well as group therapy that might focus on providing her with opportunities to establish and maintain rewarding relationships. Additionally, giving her the feedback on her successes would help her to increase her levels of self-confidence and self-efficacy. Xxx would greatly benefit from feeling and experiencing direct acceptance by others.

HIV

69. Consideration should be given to having Xxx tested for HIV antibodies given his self-report that he is involved in needle sharing and unprotected sex.
70. Consideration should be given to having Xxx tested for HIV antibodies. This is particularly recommended as Xxx's foster mother comes into contact with her blood from time to time, and should Xxx test positive, her foster mother should be encouraged to take precautions to avoid direct contact with her bodily fluids.

Individual Psychotherapy

71. Xxx should receive counseling to help stabilize his current anxiety and depression. He would also benefit from learning to view himself in a more realistic manner. Should

his condition further deteriorate, crisis intervention techniques should be utilized in order to facilitate more adaptive behavior.

72. Counseling should also focus on helping Xxx to gradually explore her angry feelings of hurt and resentment toward her parents and the rejection she feels.

73. Individual psychotherapy should also focus on helping Xxx gradually explore his angry feelings of hurt and resentment toward his father. However, given his low intellectual functioning and concrete cognitive approach to life, he is not the best candidate for insight oriented psychotherapy. The therapist should take care to approach Xxx in a supportive manner, utilizing a style he can relate to and understand.

74. Xxx might benefit from individual psychotherapy with a female therapist that can help her with positive role modeling and identification.

75. Individual psychotherapy could facilitate expression of feelings, help reduce anxiety, and enhance improved social skills.

76. Individual therapy is clearly indicated with Xxx to assist him in working through his underlying hostility, anger and insecurities and the need to be strong and powerful with others. The approach best indicated from this evaluation would be one focusing on his positive feelings toward his mother and some other members of his family. This might be a way to access affective material.

77. Counseling should help Xxx examine her personal expectations of self and significant others. She would benefit from gaining a more realistic perspective of her strengths and weaknesses. Furthermore, it is important that she become more accepting of the full range of her feelings and personal issues, thereby facilitating identity integration.

78. Xxx has a history of maladaptive behavior patterns and would benefit from being involved in individual psychotherapy.

79. Because of his high intellect and relative maturity, Xxx may benefit from individual psychotherapy which allows him to give verbal expression to his feelings of resentment,

abandonment and mistreatment. He is likely to respond well to a more dynamic approach to psychotherapy than is usual for children his age.

Medical Referral

80. Referral to his pediatrician is recommended to determine his overall level of physical health.
81. Xxx stated that she does have some difficulty with her vision. It would be important to follow through on having her eyes examined by a physician and appropriate action taken, as is deemed necessary.
82. Xxx complained of frequent headaches with the pain being localized on his right side. He stated that these occur several times weekly. It would be helpful to have him evaluated medically for this condition and appropriate action taken, if deemed necessary.
83. Xxx complained of a poor appetite, re-occurring headaches and episodic bouts of dizziness. She should undergo a thorough medical examination to rule out any organic basis to these occurrences,

Medication and or Psychiatric Consultation

84. Xxx could benefit from an ongoing review of his condition in terms of anti-psychotic medications which might assist him in controlling his reactions.
85. She should be regularly assessed by a psychiatrist to monitor her labile affect, paranoia, and psychosis to assess for psychotropic medication.
86. Continued and periodic assessment by a psychiatrist is recommended to monitor his psychiatric condition.

Molestation

87. Due to Xxx's history of being the victim of considerable sexual abuse, it would be helpful to involve him in a specialized treatment group for victims of abuse, if available.

88. Individual psychotherapy with a therapist who is experienced in treating adolescent sexual abuse issues is recommended. A great deal of Xxx's emotional difficulties can be traced to her unresolved anger related to her past molestation. This also greatly contributes to her distorted sense of self, self-mutilating behaviors, depression, and her emerging Personality Disorder traits.

89. Due to Xxx's history of parental abuse and neglect, it would be helpful to involve her in Dialectic Behavioral Therapy or any available highly structured therapy group for victims of sexual abuse. Additionally, not surprisingly, Xxx is quite self-destructive and angry toward those in authority positions and this certainly will have some bearing on how we can best meet her therapeutic needs. She is a candidate for DBT individual and re-socialization group therapy.

Neuropsychological Assessment

90. Xxx would benefit from a neuropsychological assessment to rule-out any underlying learning difficulties. She expresses concern about not being able to do well in school and has further difficulties replicating on the Bender drawings.

91. Xxx should be referred for neuropsychological testing to determine whether his poor performance on the Bender Gestalt test is indicative of organic brain dysfunction.

92. Xxx should be referred for neuropsychological assessment and testing in order to determine if organic impairment may be indicated by her verbal-performance discrepancy on the WAIS-R.

93. There were clear and sufficient indications to warrant a thorough neuropsychological evaluation of this individual.

94. A neuropsychological assessment is recommended for Xxx to rule out the possibility of organic impairment and/or learning disability.

Oppositional

95. Xxx needs to be assisted in examining the underlying sources of his defiance and resistance to authority. He needs to be able to comply with authority without feeling unduly deprived, demeaned or otherwise threatened.

96. Xxx's parents should be encouraged to take a behavioral management class that will equip them with greater skill in managing her difficult behavior. Furthermore, when Xxx becomes obstinate, her parents might try addressing the underlying emotion by acknowledging it and using behavioral consequences such as 'time-out."

97. Xxx's educational placement should be evaluated to determine if he is in the most appropriate educational setting. Given his longstanding emotional disturbance which has manifested itself in lying, stealing, bullying, and defiance toward authority figures, it can be surmised that his emotional condition has significantly interfered with his ability to achieve commensurate with his intellectual capabilities. Thus, he would benefit from a SED setting geared towards meeting the needs of students with emotional disturbance.

Peers and Relationships

98. Xxx needs to be aware of her tendency to be influenced by peers and how she has allowed them to define her self-concept and involve her in negative behaviors which result in self-defeating patterns.

99. It is recommended that treatment staff work with Xxx to identify his areas of personal strength and those in need of improvement. He lacks the ability to develop a more consolidated, positively balanced view of himself. Therefore he may be overly reliant on the reactions of others to determine his self-worth. Assist him in gaining greater independence in both his thoughts and actions, promoting greater integration and bolstering his self-esteem.

Personality Disorders

100. Xxx should be taught self management interventions to assist herself with symptom control. It is probably not a good idea to undertake deep psychodynamic psychotherapy with a borderline condition because it will promote a stormy and intense transference and she is almost certain to be moved before any kind of satisfactory stopping point can be reached.

101. Many clinicians have found the use of SSRIs to be helpful in decreasing self-harm thoughts and urges. Given his current symptom profile, Xxx may be a good candidate for medication treatment from a specialist.

Placement

102. Xxx requires continued residential and psychiatric services. It appears that he has received maximum benefit from his current residential treatment experience. Long term placement should be pursued for this individual.

103. She needs continued placement in an environment where she can experience warmth and acceptance, but where consistent limits are set on interpersonal behavior.

104. He needs continued placement in an environment where he can experience warmth and acceptance, but where consistent limits are set on interpersonal behavior. He continues to need a concrete, behaviorally oriented, structured approach that will appropriately reinforce his positive, and extinguish negative, behaviors.

105. Xxx struggles with competing desires to be both dependent and independent. It is important that she learn how to gratify her need for nurturance and at the same time feel that her need for autonomy and separateness is not being challenged.

106. Xxx continues to need placement in a structured, warm, and accepting environment where the relationship between behavior and its consequences are emphasized.

107. Xxx continues to need a great deal of structure and limits. The residential treatment program needs to continue

to reinforce positive behaviors and immediately set limits and consequences when he acts out.

108. Xxx needs clear and consistent rules and guidelines for her behavior. This is an individual who very much wants to please adults in her environment and this examiner expects that she will continue to do well at her placement.

109. Given his turbulent and abusive history, Xxx needs, and responds to, a sensibly structured living situation which rewards his appropriate behavior and which sets reasonable limits for him. Emotionally impoverished, Xxx responds rather simply and affirmatively to any success and encouragement that such an environment can offer.

110. It is recommended that Xxx continue with the group home placement and be re-evaluated in six months. He has expressed suicidal ideations in the past which should be closely monitored.

Poor Prognosis

111. Xxx's prognosis is guarded. His adjustment within the home, socially, and at school seemed to be erratic and marginal. As he faces impending emancipation, it is likely he is going to continue his questionable level of functioning. He is capable of operating at a higher level than his history would suggest. Yet emotional factors continue to impede his personal development and adaptation. It is not feasible to expect integral changes in his personality and coping style before he turns eighteen. Efforts within the home should be addressed toward emancipation. Given his age, it is important that he be assisted in clarifying his education, vocational and social objectives. He needs help in learning how to set realistic goals, implementing a plan and sustaining his motivation until his aims are achieved.

112. The MMPI test results indicate the emergence of psychotic thought processes. Xxx should receive a follow-up evaluation within 3-6 months from another clinician to confirm these test findings and offer a second option.

113. During the assessment process, Xxx clearly did not appear to put forth his best effort. There were also indications of malingering and self-sabotaging behaviors. Given his history of academic underachievement and emerging conduct disturbances, there is a clear indication that Xxx may need referrals for a SED educational format and ongoing psychotherapy.

Refer for Speech/Language Assessment

114. A number of aphasic signs have been identified; more specialized testing is required to assess their nature from an educational perspective so that appropriate remediation can be undertaken. Xxx would benefit from assessment by a speech-language pathologist to identify the specific nature of her expressive/receptive language problems, and to determine whether she needs a specially designed curriculum to remedy them.

115. Xxx has a noticeable lisp that has inhibited him in social settings. He could benefit from a speech and language assessment as well as speech therapy as part of his school curriculum.

Self-Esteem

116. Individual counseling focused on development of positive self-concept and resolution of psychosexual issues is recommended.

117. It is important for treatment staff to be alert to signs of sexual acting out. Xxx may be oriented toward establishing her attachments to males, in part, as a way to establish a surrogate paternal figure. While an interest in male peers is clearly appropriate for someone Xxx'x age, unresolved family conflicts may interfere with establishing appropriate interpersonal ties.

118. It would be important in the therapy setting to examine Xxx's expectations of himself and others. He often seems to feel disappointed and angry when dealing with others. This may stem in part from the fact that his expectations

are unrealistic and ultimately lead to Xxx being disappointed because he views others as failing him.

119. Xxx needs help building her self-esteem. It may be helpful to find activities that she excels in to help boost her sense of accomplishment and mastery. For example exposure to skills such as public speaking, and leadership training would be helpful.

120. It would be important to ensure that Xxx has adequate intellectual challenges academically so that he is not bored in the regular classroom. It is also recommended that Xxx be exposed to cultural and educational activities that will expand and enrich his already strong intellect.

121. For the immediate future, encouraging her academic achievement, particularly in mathematics, is recommended. She would benefit from some type of a career awareness in which she could use her superior intellectual abilities.

122. Treatment staff should work with Xxx to help him begin to develop a more integrated self-concept and to bolster his feelings of little personal self-worth.

123. It would be worthwhile to continue to encourage him in his sports pursuits. It is important for his identity development and self-esteem to have an area where he can distinguish himself and feel special.

124. It is recommended that treatment staff work with Xxx to identify her areas of personal strengths and those in need of improvement. She lacks the ability to develop a more consolidated, positively balanced view of herself. Therefore, she may be overly reliant on the reactions of others to determine her self-worth. Assist her in gaining greater independence in both her thoughts and actions, promoting greater identity integration and bolster her self-esteem.

Safe Sex

125. Xxx should think twice before beginning sexual relations with a new partner. He should first discuss his past partners, history of STDs, and drug use.

126. It would be important to explore Xxx's sexual identity and involvement with males. As Xxx matures, she would benefit from nonphysical needs, identifying other ways to gratify her desires for affiliation and acceptance that do not necessarily involve sexual behavior or acting out.

127. Xxx experiences residual feelings in reference to long-standing issues of separation and loss, and abandonment from his family upbringing. Insecurities and interpersonal ambivalence stemming from these times continue to influence his self-worth and interpersonal relationships. Therefore, it would be of some use to encourage Xxx to express himself in this regard, and learn how these issues might influence how he feels about himself and how he gets along with others.

128. Xxx should be encouraged to always use condoms of latex or polyurethane—not natural materials. The Centers for Disease Control and Prevention (CDC) recommends that latex condoms with or without spermicides, should be used to help prevent sexual transmission of HIV.

129. Xxx should have annual Pap tests and tests for STDs. She should be aware of her partner's body and look for signs of sores, blisters, rash, or discharge.

Special Education

130. Xxx should be placed in a special education setting. He definitely qualifies for S.E.D. classification given his long-standing behavioral problems and labile behavior, which has significantly impaired his ability to function in a regular classroom setting. He would benefit from a highly structured, one-on-one setting with direct supervision. This would allow for greater control over competing and distracting stimuli than a regular classroom and help to meet the needs he exhibits as a result of his behavioral and emotional disturbance.

131. This individual is experiencing a sense of helplessness and hopelessness which render her quite depressed, and as a result a special education setting is advised.

132. This individual is experiencing blocking, confused thinking and slowed cognitions due to his clinical depression, and as a result direct classroom supervision is advised.

133. Xxx's educational placement should be re-evaluated to determine if he is in the most appropriate educational setting. Given his longstanding emotional disturbance which has manifested itself in lying, stealing, criminal activity and defiance towards authority figures, it can be surmised that his emotional condition has significantly interfered with his ability to achieve commensurate with his intellectual capabilities. Thus, he would benefit from a special education setting geared towards meeting the needs of students with emotional disturbances.

134. The current test findings suggest that Xxx may have difficulty functioning within a regular classroom setting. Her variable motivation, inconsistent cognitive capabilities, and instability in mood interfere with her capacity to progress academically. She should be considered for placement in a special educational classroom where she could benefit from a greater structure and supervision.

135. He is in need of a small structured learning environment with direct supervision to help reduce the negative effects of his learning disabilities and the disruptive effects of his emotional disturbance. A special education format will provide greater control over competing and distracting stimuli than a regular classroom setting, as well as to create a more personally interesting and stimulating educational environment.

136. Since Xxx is not interested in reading standard written materials, she could benefit from a language experience approach to teaching this skill in which she creates materials for herself to read. She dictates stories and the teacher writes the story.

Social Skills

137. Xxx needs to develop improved social skills with peers in order to compensate for his sense of inadequacy. Social skills training and group psychotherapy which empha-

sizes role playing and application of skills could promote social confidence.

138. Xxx's social skills need to be enhanced. It is important that she begin to learn how to establish and sustain reciprocal ties with peers and adults alike.

139. Given his background and lack of appropriate and consistent parenting, it would be beneficial for Xxx to learn how to get the attention and affection that he requires in ways that do not involve negative acting out. This would enhance his social skills and means of relating both to peers and adults alike. At present, he has a need for external supervision to help him set realistic limits in his dealings with others.

140. Help Xxx become aware of how she can facilitate communication by modeling appropriate interpersonal interactions. For example, demonstrate how to acknowledge hearing and understanding a statement by repeating it. Then model appropriate responses, taking into consideration the non-verbal and verbal cues which may be implied or overtly stated.

141. Conflict resolution strategies can help Xxx learn to negotiate, defuse, avoid or appropriately confront problematic interpersonal interactions.

142. Providing Xxx with the behavioral learning and feedback that is necessary to put his feelings into words, rather than acting them out, would be of great benefit. It appears that he has been rewarded in the past for immature behaviors and has not learned or been rewarded for more age appropriate behaviors. Providing him with the opportunity to practice social skills as well as giving him constant feedback would help bring them to a more age-appropriate level.

143. Xxx tends to project her feelings of hostility onto others. Her peer relationships are strained. She would benefit from participation in group therapy, where in part, the focus should be on increasing communication and the encouragement of empathy.

144. Help Xxx improve communication by helping him verbalize his feelings. When he withdraws from social interac-

tions he withholds his feelings and likely increases his depression.

Suicide

145. Although Xxx appears depressed, her suicidal ideation or intent is low. However, treatment staff should work with Xxx in helping her identify alternative ways to respond should the urge to hurt herself arise in the future.
146. Xxx's intent to kill himself is low, yet he did speak of vague suicidal ideations. It would be important to deal with his feelings of loss and anger in reference to his family situation. Moreover, he needs to find alternative ways to deal with his emotions when they surface, rather than entertain the thought of killing himself.
147. Because this individual is experiencing a sense of helplessness and hopelessness which render her quite depressed, her suicidal ideations and/or attempts need to be addressed.

Tutoring and Educational Support

148. Academic remediation is clearly indicated which would best take the form of individual tutoring, perhaps with another, older adolescent who is more skilled in academic pursuits.
149. Xxx would benefit from tutoring, especially for subjects that she has difficulty understanding. As she wants to do better in school, it appears that such tutoring might provide her with some support.
150. Xxx would benefit from tutoring. As he wants to do better in school it appears that such tutoring might provide him with support.

Glossary

AA—Alcoholics Anonymous. A fellowship with the goal of helping oneself and others recover from alcoholism

ACA—Adult Children of Alcoholics -12 step program or support group for individuals who grew up in alcoholic or dysfunctional households

Affect—emotion, feeling, mood

Anger Management—techniques and exercises by which an individual can control or reduce an excessively angered state

Assertiveness Training—finding a midway between aggression and passivity

Atypical Depression—out of the ordinary depressive symptoms

Bender Gestalt Test—a psychological test used to evaluate visual motor maturity and to assess neurological function

Balanced Lifestyle—a lifestyle in which the subject has control of their behavior and chooses behaviors that are generally moderate

Blocking- disruption or inhibition of thought processes

Borderline- emotionally unstable personality

Clarification—exploration of data that are vague or contradictory

Confrontation—drawing the individual's attention to data that is discrepant or outside of their Awareness

Cognitive Behavioral Therapy—encourages the individual to recognize and change distorted thinking that worsens symptoms

Chemical Dependency—illness or disease characterized by addiction to a mind altering Chemical

DBT—Dialectic Behavior Therapy is a system of therapy designed to treat Borderline Personality Disorders

Decompensation—functional deterioration of a previously working system

Delusion- a belief that is maintained despite evidence to the contrary

DSM-IV—The Diagnostic and Statistical Manual of Mental Disorders—Fourth Edition

Dysphoria—moderate depressive mood

Family-Focused Therapy—educates family members so they can better support an individual's recovery

Hallucinations—hearing, seeing or smelling things others can't

Ideations—notion in the mind or belief

Identification—the process whereby the individual internalizes aspects of important others

Impulsive—acting without first thinking about the action

Interpretation—giving meaning to the link between the individual's unmet needs and actions

Intrapsychic—within a person

Labile affect—marked by rapid mood shifts

Lisp—a speech impediment also know as stigmatism

Maladaptive Behavior Patterns—patterns of behavior likely to produce so much psychic distress that therapy is necessary

MMPI—Minnesota Multiphasic Personality Inventory, a widely used instrument assessing personality and symptoms of distress

NA—Narcotic Anonymous. 12 step meetings or groups sessions that encourage sobriety

Neurosis—mental disorder characterized by high levels of anxiety but no impairment in reality testing

Paranoia—having unfound suspicions and beliefs that one is being plotted against

Psychosis—grossly impaired reality testing such as symptoms of delusions and hallucinations

Relapse—a total reversal of "old" behavioral patterns

Rorschach—A projective personality test where the stimuli ink blots are assumed to be neutral and what the individual sees in the blots are a product of his own experiences and and perceptual orientation projected onto the cards

SED—an educational format geared for the severely emotionally disturbed child

SSRIs—Selective Serotonin Reuptake Inhibitors. A class of anti depressive medications used as a first line treatment for depression

Time-out—a behavioral technique used as a consequence for negative or disruptive behaviors

WAIS-R- Wechsler Adult Intelligence Scale—Revised

www.ingramcontent.com/pod-product-compliance
Lightning Source LLC
Chambersburg PA
CBHW060013300526

45794CB00003B/1187